Cathy

You are such a blessing. Keep your vision burning —

Love,

Barbara

Eph 2:10

THE BLANK CANVAS

By

BARBARA LACHANCE

For Worldwide Distribution, Printed in the U.S.A.

ISBN: 978-0-615-458786

The Blank Canvas

By Barbara G. Lachance

Published by Barbara G. Lachance

Copyright 2011 — Barbara G. Lachance
Barbra@generationalsolutionsllc.com

www.barbaralachanceministries.org

Cover Design by **Tiffany Lively**
lively.entertainment@gmail.com

ACKNOWLEDGEMENTS

Without the help of my husband, Gerry, whose encouragement kept me focused; this book couldn't have been accomplished. I want to thank Paul Taylor, my friend and colleague, who planted the idea of sharing my love of painting with others, causing me to become serious about writing the Blank Canvas. My pastor Marios Ellinas, who was a tremendous support with his words, reminding me of the gifting and talents that God wanted me to use for the good of the kingdom. Rhonda Harder, who worked with me, putting flowers around the words, diligently editing this book and finally, I want to give my appreciation to Michael Sullo, my art teacher, who believed in the talent God had given me, helped me fine-tune it, and gave me the confidence to say, "I am an artist."

FOREWORD

Barbara Lachance is God's masterpiece; and so is *The Blank Canvas*. A few months ago, I had the opportunity to have breakfast with Barbara. While enjoying juice, omelets and pumpkin apple pancakes, I asked Barbara to share her life's story with me. I wanted to identify the factors contributing to the wonderful peace, love, and clarity I feel whenever I visit the Lachance home. I asked questions about Barbara's walk with God, her amazing relationship with her husband Gerry, raising their biological and adopted children, and the core values of their household, ministries, and businesses. Barbara was so gracious to open up her heart and share. By the time she was finished, her story had inspired me so much, I wanted to be alone with God somewhere so I could weep in His presence, I was so touched. Truly, the Lord has been forming a masterpiece out of the yielded and consecrated life of His servant, Barbara. *The Blank Canvas* is birthed from and representative of Barbara's phenomenal life-story, her impeccable character, her outstanding insight, and her deep understanding of God and His ways.

The book clearly defines and explains the process by which God masterfully combines His unending love with His infinite creativity to form God-glorifying "paintings" out of our lives. The prose is crystal clear, and Barbara's analogies are powerful, stirring up an even greater desire in us to encounter and grow in relationship with the Master of the masterpiece.

At a time when much of the brokenness in our world can be attributed to individuals' misunderstood, lost or stolen identities as beloved children of our heavenly Father, *The Blank Canvas* is a most timely proclamation of a Truth that heals, encourages, and inspires.

I am fully confident each reader will be impacted greatly. I honor Barbara for blessing and adding value to our lives, both through *The Blank Canvas* and the amazing God-journey from which this book is derived!

Marios Ellinas
Lead Pastor
Valley Shore Assembly of God
Old Saybrook, Connecticut

ENDORSEMENTS

Picking Up The Brush

The book you are about to read was once an unpainted corner on the canvas of the life of Barbara Lachance. Its' composition was intertwined with that part of the overall painting that already existed. The fact that the painting continuously evolves in a multimedia fashion attests to the reality that it is not the work of one mortal alone but a joint effort. Two craftsmen, working hand in hand, have completed and will ultimately finish the canvas. In the end the painting will be a masterpiece compiled of the suggestions and directions of the all-creating hand of God and the hand of the apprentice who stayed in harmony. WHY? Why put on paper the personal and private experiences of Barbara Lachance? There are three explanations:

FIRST: You, all mankind, and I emanated from the same Master artist who paints only masterworks. By reflecting on "a work in progress" belonging to another, we can gain a more perfect understanding of the brushwork that defines our own life's painting. And through this contemplation, realize that no matter what the critics review is our painting is a masterpiece.

SECOND: Just as a visit to a museum of modern art requires that you open your mind to new ideas, this book demands the same consideration. By allowing yourself the luxury to stretch and imagine, the book contents will widen your understanding of the intentions of the master artist.

THIRD: HORIZONE LINES, VANISHING POINTS, AND PERSPECTIVE are the heart and soul of any painted canvas. It is sometimes difficult to visualize these elements and we sometimes get lost in a torrent of construction lines. As any earthly art professor will tell you when this happens step back, move the light source, and view the work of others. This dissertation "The Blank Canvas" will encourage you to do just that. By the act of viewing life as a blank canvas we can see more clearly the composition we are creating. When we lose our perspective, look toward the master and it will be restored. When our horizon becomes obscured we can change the light source from self-lit to divinely illuminate. When the vanishing points fail to assist us to keep things at bay, we will remember that this is not a one person Masterpiece. Like Michelangelo and the ceiling it takes many workers to complete a massive undertaking. And like Michelangelo the "well done good and faithful servant," Come now; lay down thy brush and rest!

Dr. Michael Sullo
Independent Professor of Fine Art

Table of Contents

INTRODUCTION

About ten years ago on one of my leisurely walks, I realized I was in front of our local art association. It was located in a beautiful building sitting on the shore of the Mystic River. Something seemed to be telling me to go in and inquire about taking lessons. As I opened the door to enter I kept saying to myself, "What am I doing? What will I say?" However the impulse was strong, so in I went. I met the director and told her what was on my mind. She said the best thing to do was to meet with an art teacher and discuss the possibilities. As I talked with the instructor I told her a part of me really wanted to paint. I couldn't draw and the only things I had ever painted were the walls of my house. She laughed and told me I was the kind of student she would enjoy having. And yes, she could teach me to paint. She then gave me the supply list. I spent a small fortune on the easel, oil paint canvases, brushes and other supplies. However, the expense of the supplies became insignificant when my teacher told me the second week of class that she could teach technique to anyone but I seemed to have a natural talent. I was thrilled! I couldn't wait to get home and tell my husband.

"God gave me the gift of painting," I announced as I came through the door. As I related my experience of the day my husband and I realized this gift was yet another way I could share God's message. At that time neither of us had any idea just how this new gift would be used or what a wonderful illustration God had planned. As I moved forward with my art lessons I learned various techniques and fine-tuned my own style. God began to reveal to me the beautiful way I could share His message through painting.

In this bookl, I want to share the painting techniques I most enjoy, and, illustrate for you the beautiful comparison of a blank canvas with a life journey. God is the artist. He is painting each life as a masterpiece. My good friend and colleague, Dr. Paul Taylor wrote an article for his blog, The Voice of Destiny, that caught my attention.

In the article he mentioned that God wanted him (Paul) to come to Him as a blank canvas. In other words, God didn't want Paul to come before Him with a preconceived agenda but come with an open mind and heart to hear what he had to say. When I read the words "blank canvas" I became very curious.

I would like to share with you how I enhanced my relationship with God through my love of art and learning the process of painting. I would also like for you to see how my closeness with the Father has allowed me to see my talent for art as part of the destiny He planned for me.

This booklet tells my story of using a God given talent to draw me closer to my Heavenly Father. It is also about a Father's response to a child who wants to have an intimate relationship with one of His children. By acknowledging His gift and using it to glorify Him, I have learned how to go forth in life fulfilling my purpose and doing my part to create change in the world around me. I have told my story using the tools of Impressionist painting. I hope my experience will encourage you to look for your talent and lead you to a closer walk with God. Accepting our God given talents and utilizing them, while praying for guidance, helps us to understand the uniqueness of our lives and how we fit into the beautiful masterpiece God is painting every day.

I hope you enjoy reading my story as much as I enjoy sharing it with you. For more information about The Blank Canvas please check out my website at www.barbaralachanceministries.org

Barbara G. Lachance

CHAPTER 1

THE BLANK CANVAS

~ *We are God's masterpiece. He has created us anew in Christ Jesus, so we can do the good things He planned for us long ago. (NTL)* ~

Ephesians 2:10

It was 5:00 a.m. My room was still dark. As I lay nestled beneath soft, warm blankets in a cozy bed, my thoughts turned to my interest in artistic painting. I smiled as I realized God was sending me a message. During the early morning hours, before dawn, God and I often spent time talking and planning my day. Today it seemed I was going to focus on my painting.

In recent months, before this early morning message from God, I had thoughts that I might use my love for painting to enhance my ministry. It wasn't an occasional thought, it was a thought I was having every day. Throughout my ministry, my focus had been speaking, pastoral counseling, writing and prayer. Painting was a different medium for me. I was excited to have a new way of sharing my testimony and my love for God. Furthermore, it was obvious God was leading in this, which meant it would be both exciting and personal.

"Thank you Father, show me the way." I whispered.

Comforted by my thoughts, and accepting that my day would find me exploring painting techniques, I gave into the temptation to go to the kitchen and get myself a cup of coffee. I was headed to the couch, coffee in hand to relax and savor the beginning of the new day, when the words BLANK CANVAS appeared on my mind like a neon sign. Quietly following were almost audible words, "Barbara, what do you need to paint?"

Somewhat startled by this revelation, my first impulse was to utilize my "God given" somewhat sassy sense of humor and answer, "Don't you already know that?"

However, feeling God's presence in the room and realizing He was about to share an important lesson with me I did not act on my frivolous impulse.

Quickly recalling recent conversations with my art teacher on the techniques of Impressionist painting, 101 if you will, I began listing the tools needed: easel, brushes, charcoal, paint, and rags.

"And a blank canvas." His voice was loud and clear. "Yes Father, and a blank canvas." I replied. Where was God leading me? What did He want me to see in this illustration?

Sitting quietly and waiting, it occurred to me we were all blank canvases in the beginning. Thought out long before we were born, tools assembled, holding the paintbrush, standing in front of an easel, we were going to provide God each hour, each day and each year that we lived, the colors to make our blank canvas a masterpiece. Consider how the following information shows the variety in paintings compared to variety of human beings. Paintings are traditionally divided into five categories or 'genres' if you prefer.

1. Historical Paintings (works with a message or moralistic content) possibly compared to people who are afraid to make changes. They were brought up with certain religious beliefs, and new ideas, especially where their faith is concerned makes them uneasy. They are more comfortable living in the past, and are afraid of change.

2. Portraits (individual, group or self-portraits) I'll just step out on a limb and say these might possibly be the people who always want to be seen wherever they might be or whatever they might be doing. This type of person is not afraid to lead. They are comfortable with people and are the first to step up when needed.

3. Genre-paintings (everyday scenes) Good solid people. They are there every day doing their thing and not wanting any praise or attention. I've heard this type of person referred to as worker bees; they make the world go around.

4. Landscapes (self explanatory) this would be the people with color flying in every direction all the time, taking advantage of every day and every hour to just live, and the final category.

5. Still life (also self-explanatory) we all know these people. For some still waters run deep. And for others they might be the people who go to church each week, sit in the same pew, sing the same songs, say the same prayers and go home. Perhaps out of habit, their time with God has become more of a weekly routine than a true walk with the Father. And in their contentment, they may not be looking for much more.

As God stands ready to paint our personal canvas He allows us to provide the colors, techniques and the style. He leads us throughout our life but does not interfere with our free will allowing us to choose what colors He will use to paint our individual masterpieces. He creates each one of us unique; our portrait won't be like anyone else's.

Types of paintings and well-known artist you might be familiar with are: Abstract: Jackson Pollock; Impressionism: Claude Monet; or Cubism: Pablo Picasso.

My personal preference is Impressionism. If you've ever looked at books with Impressionist paintings, such as Monet, or been fortunate enough to visit his gardens in France, you can actually compare the real thing with the painting as you feel yourself walking into the picture while you are viewing it.

As I walk you through the process, you'll soon understand why: The style allows the artist to think of what he or she wants to paint, plan the placement and begin with an outline. The outline is done with charcoal, and then the color called yellow ochre is applied over the charcoal. This process won't distort the purity of other colors it enhances the outline making it easier to see. The artist then tones the canvass from the dark point to the light, and outlines with two bold colors, dark ultramarine and alisrium crimson, to bring the picture into focus on the canvas. Finally, he applies pure color to the picture with a process called, crosshatching. The strokes are gently applied in the motion of the cross.

God began to show me just why I chose Impressionism and how the process is much like drawing a life canvas. The charcoal outlines our lives, allowing stages to be added as we live and grow in

Christ. The yellow ochre works as the Holy Spirit, blending all the colors but not distorting them or interfering, as in our free will. The toning process (also compared to the work of the Holy Spirit) goes into the darkest places of our past and brings the darkness into light, turning them into purity and holiness. The two bold colors bring out the true picture of character and design. And finally, God's hand gently brushes the canvas with the stroke of the cross. Everything in life begins and ends at the cross.

When I accepted Jesus as my Savior, my life changed. My desire was to serve Him in every way possible. That early morning conversation with God that revealed the correlation between Impressionism and my personal walk with Him brought a new awareness of how intimate my relationship with God had become. The entire experience changed my life forever.

Paintings can't be rushed. It takes discipline, patience and time. The more you paint the better you become. But you never rush. Anything worthwhile is worth waiting for. Even though God knows the end from the beginning, He doesn't interfere and He doesn't rush.

One of the other things I like about painting in oils is if you make a mistake you can start over and not ruin your picture. How many times do you think God starts over with our blank canvas? Fortunately for us, Jesus made it possible for Him to start over as many times as needed. All of our imperfections are covered again and again by Jesus at the cross.

All paintings are eventually finished. As human beings our lives eventually come to an end, at least here on earth. God knows when we are born what that end will be. He gives us every tool we need to add color to our canvas of life, and is with us every step of the way, adding it to complete our picture. While I can now call myself an artist, I am certainly not an expert in the art field. When I look at a beautiful painting I am amazed at how the artist can place the subject on a canvas and capture its beauty. Since taking art lessons I now look at paintings differently. I look at the subject of the painting. I often wonder why the artist chose to do the particular piece. And, I often try and think of what emotion the artist must have been feeling when he painted the picture. I see colors I've never seen before and often experience emotions that seem to come from nowhere while viewing a painting. In each piece I see the hand of God. I've never met a true artist that doesn't fully realize their talent to express themselves through paint was a gift from the living God.

My husband and I often tell our audiences, in the seminars we conduct, that God has a destiny for each person. God wants each of us to leave our footprint on earth. To do so, we must prayerfully search God's word for guidance and follow His leading to be sure we are on the right path. We believe that when you receive a revelation regarding your destiny God will show you the way as you begin the process. As when you start a painting, you have an idea and an outline, you then work out the details as you go along.

When we begin our journey, faith is a huge factor. To discover our true path we must first ask ourselves some pointed questions:

1. Where are my interests?
2. What tugs at my heart?
3. What are my talents and gifts?
4. What do I want from life?
5. What circumstances have brought me to where I am in life?
6. Who are the people that influence me and affirm me?
7. And what do I already know that brings me fulfillment and delight?

If you are honest with yourself in answering these questions you will receive revelation from God, gaining knowledge, sound judgment, understanding, and wisdom when looking for your destiny. Are you ready to paint your picture? Draw your vision:

> *Write the vision and make it plain on tablets, that he may run who reads it. For the vision is yet for an appointed time, but at the end it will speak, and it will not lie. Though it tarries, wait for it,*

because it will surely come, it will not tarry.
Habakkuk 2:2-3.

Questions for Reflection:

1. How do you imagine your canvas if you could see it today?
2. What step in the painting process is God working on now with your life canvas?
3. Has God had to start over on your canvas since He started painting?

CHAPTER 2

PREPARING TO PAINT

~ There is no fear in love; but perfect love casts out fear, because fear involves torment. But he who fears has not been made perfect in love. ~

1 John 4:18

So do we dare anticipate the final master-piece? Each experience of life provides God with the vibrant colors needed to make your personal canvas all it was meant to be? In order to do this, you have to put aside your fear. Fear is rooted in pride. When we fear we are saying God doesn't have the power, to change our circumstances. (But Scripture tells us that God has all the power and the authority.) Our desire is to continue doing it on our own. It is not easy to let go and let God, to do so you must have faith.

Making the choice to move ahead without fear is not easy. However, I'm here to tell you that is exactly what I've learned to do. Through faith, as my relationship has grown with God I am no longer afraid to follow His leading even if I don't know exactly where it will lead. As I stay focused on Him, He directs my every step. I set aside time each morning devoted just to God. Not only do I talk with

Him, I sit quietly and listen carefully in the silence that follows. His leading may come as a thought or a Bible verse remembered. Whatever God has to say to me or however He chooses to say it, I want to be sure that I am able to receive it.

Time spent with God helps reinforce our faith. We talk with Him and let Him know our every need. We learn patience by waiting for His answer. God answers every prayer! Maybe not exactly when we want Him to or how we want Him to but He does answer. The amazing thing is His answer is always the right answer. Are you willing to trust God? Is your faith growing? Are you able to be patient and wait for His answer, the right answer?

Let's say you are working with an art teacher and you're painting your first painting for an upcoming art show. You've expressed your desire to do an Impressionist painting and your instructor has approved. You're enjoying yourself following the steps outlined until suddenly you decide to add something rather abstract. Your teacher walks by and sees the unusual addition to your painting. He tries to explain to you why it won't work and tells you to go back to the original plan. You are now faced with a choice: going forward with your change in place (remember it's your painting) knowing it isn't going to end well and you could possibly be thrown out of the show altogether, or returning to the original plan, completing your piece as approved and possibly winning first prize. Remember, with oil paint you can correct your mistakes and no one will know!

Our relationship and communication with God directs us in His ways. If we listen to God and trust Him, our canvas will be exactly as He planned. And, we can trust it will be a masterpiece of His making.

When I first started painting there was always the apprehension that I would do it wrong. All the old negative self-talk would stream through my mind like a flood. Putting aside these thoughts wasn't easy. This is when I would recall my teacher saying, "Don't be afraid. You can do it. It will come back to you. Have faith."

My recent thirst to use my love of art in my ministry was from God. He was calling me to be that canvas and work with the Holy Spirit for knowledge, understanding and wisdom of the process. He wanted me to deal with the process in order to complete the destiny He has for my life. How else could I share the information through my ministry and explain the message to those I minister to. He wanted to paint a beautiful picture and show me the comparison to a life canvas in the process. In order for Him to do this, I would need to allow Him to work out the process in me.

Painting takes discipline. I have to want to set time aside out of my day to devote just for the art. There can be no distractions. I have to be totally focused to create the desired finished picture. As I fine tune my techniques and see my progress I start to look forward to the time spent in front of the easel. My anticipation of reaching my goal fills me with excitement.

It is much the same with prayer and time with God. The more time we spend in communicating with God, the more time we will want to communicate with God. The more we study and learn of Him, the more we will want to know Him on an intimate level.

My prayer life started some forty years ago. When I first started praying God gave me everything I asked for. It didn't matter if I wanted my lost dog to return home, my sick child to be healed or my husband to get a new job. It was a season in my life that God seemed to be spoiling me like a little child to develop a faith that could not be shaken. I knew if I asked God for something He would answer. I still believe that deep understanding of what He has prepared for us.

> *What eye has not seen and ear has not heard and has not entered into the heart of man [all that] God has prepared [made and keeps ready] for those who love Him [who hold Him in affectionate reverence, promptly obeying Him and gratefully recognizing the benefits He has*

bestowed.] Yet to us God has unveiled and revealed them by and through His Spirit, for the [Holy] Spirit searches diligently, exploring and examining everything, even sounding the profound and bottomless things of God [the divine] counsels and things hidden and beyond man's scrutiny].
1 Corinthians 2:9-10 (AMP)

Just as it takes sensitivity to paint, one must develop spiritual sensitivity to have an intimate relationship with God. Sensitivity comes from getting to know God on a personal level. To do this, when you spend time with God you must ask Him to help you search the scriptures for His instruction. Let him know the desires of your heart. You must learn to look for Him in all you do and listen for His voice in making decisions. God's deep secrets are not known in the natural realm, but are revealed by His Spirit. God wants to show us what He has prepared for us and we won't see or hear unless we devote time to focus on Him and let Him lead in our daily lives.

When I start a picture and I am into the process, I often step back, study it, see if there is anything I want to change or something I can improve on, and then implement my findings. Patience helps keep us faithful to God's leading. It keeps us focused on our goal so we won't lose heart or hope. There are challenges for us in every aspect of our lives. It is up to us to meet them and work our way through them with God's help.

Sometimes these challenges are painful. However, He never leaves us and He will always lead us through if we only learn to be patient and trusting.

I had a beautiful, precious daughter named Gretchen, who happened to be severely handi-capped. She has gone home to be with the Lord. Our comfort comes from knowing she has been made whole. I smile as I see her waiting to welcome us with open arms when we enter heaven. This was something she could never do here on earth. Taking care of her taught me patience. Working with her mandated an atmosphere that couldn't be rushed; her care, to be done lovingly and kindly took a tremendous amount of time. Time and patience were the easy parts of Gretchen's care. Working with her, moving her, bathing her, changing her were all very physical activities. It simply wasn't possible to rush. Patience came naturally through my love and concern as a mother. I was busy when we were together but it seemed time flew. Where love is concerned there is no rush.

God's love for us comes naturally. We are His children. He doesn't rush us. He leads us and cares for us as He shows us the way each day of our lives. When we have to sit and wait patiently for something, or someone, it takes a whole different set of skills. Waiting on God, being quiet, listening carefully and remaining calm while you wait is a difficult process that is learned over time. If we can learn to wait patiently the results are astounding.

Waiting for God to show us the way is like anticipating the finish of the picture we are painting. You know what you hope it will look like, however not rushing and remaining calm will guarantee the result you are looking for. Often times you discover it may not be exactly what you had pictured in your mind, however because you were patient and took your time it has turned out even better than anticipated.

Many times peoples' prayers are only about asking God for something. They forget to thank Him for the blessings He has already given them. People want to equate God with a magician. They ask Him for something and expect Him to magically pull their answers out of His hat, so to speak, and presto, they are good to go!

So, how do you find Him? Well, first of all, He's always there. He's waiting for you to miss Him and invite Him back into your life. It all goes back to believing. Believing is the same as having faith.

Without faith it is impossible to please God, because anyone who comes to Him

must believe that He exists and that He
reward those who earnestly seek Him.
Hebrews 11:6

Since my early days of being a Christian, I have always spent time with God in prayer. As my communication with God deepened I wanted everyone to know how prayer could enrich his or her daily devotions with God. In 1999 I founded the Connecticut House of Prayer and have been active in spreading the word of personal and corporate communication with God. In this process God has shown me that discipline turns to desire and desire turns to delight.

So discipline is important. You set aside time to commune with God. As you grow in your relationship and once again feel His comfort and calm your discipline turns to desire. You will feel you can't wait to wake up for a new day and the quiet time you spend with the Father before dawn. Or you will look forward to getting the kids off to school, sitting down with your Bible and reading the message He has chosen for that day. That's how desire comes into the picture.

Life won't be perfect but you will see the change. You'll smile more. Little things won't seem to bother you. And, you will want to spend as much time as possible communing with God. You will find yourself talking to God in a way you've never experienced before.

I have learned to be patient as my relationship has grown. If I stay focused on Him, He directs my every step. I thank Him for His love and patience as I continue my journey and I wait quietly and patiently as God answers my prayers. Maybe not exactly when I want Him to, or how I want Him to, but He does answer. The amazing thing is His answer is always the right answer.

Are you willing to trust God? Are you in a place where you can let your faith grow in Him? Or, are you going to venture forth and try it on your own? Through painting God has taught me with faith, discipline and patience I can have an intimate, sensitive relationship with Him.

As I once again thought back to my early morning conversation with God, I wondered if I had received and understood the message He had meant for me. I asked God to give me insight into this entire message and thanked Him for using art for such a beautiful illustration into my personal life canvas. I believe He has answered the question.

God's illustration through painting is very clear to me now. My masterpiece is not finished. I believe my canvas is not full. God is working with me to complete His masterpiece. I have often said that each life is unique. Some are content to give God material for a 9 X 12. Others will use a space of 11 X 14. And then there are those of us hoping for at least a 24 x 36, or perhaps a wall mural. I want to be all that I can be.

I want God to have all the colors He needs to make my life picture all it was meant to be. I strive each day to add color to my life painting and become one of God's true masterpieces.

How about you, have you asked God to show you the colors still needed to finish your masterpiece? Do you know what your finished portrait will look like? Are you providing God with pure colors for your canvas of life? This is the place to start by seeking God and asking Him for insight into the colors of your life.

So, we know we need to pray for guidance. We know we need faith, patience, discipline and the proper tools for our life to provide God with all He needs to paint our picture. Now we just need to create our masterpiece.

Questions for Reflection

1. Do I take time to communicate with God each day?
2. Do I have the discipline, faith and patience to let God paint my masterpiece without interfering?
3. What style of painting do you think God has chosen for your personal portrait?

CHAPTER 3

THE CONSTRUCTION
CREATING THE DRAWING

~ Before you were born, your end result was already deposited within you. God did not place birth and death in your womb. He placed the discovery of a Divine Word, and He also placed the result of that word within you. He created your beginning and end, not just being born and dying. ~

Undrai Fizer

I mpressionism is my favorite style to paint. Impressionism is a theory or style of painting originating and developed in France during the 1870s. It is characterized by concentration on the visual effects of the moment, especially using the influence of light and colors.

The construction, or creative process, of a painting should remain free; this is one of the first rules of Impressionism. Too much detail will cause you to lose something in the process. The charcoal that is used in placing the outline is very fine. This is where the proper care of your instruments and tools becomes very important. Having the appropriate tools in good condition will enable you to start with the correct foundation for the painting. Before starting to paint, you draw the constructions lines then wipe off the excess charcoal. Simply take a clean rag and wipe very lightly over the canvas so there is only a faint line visible to the eye. This acts as a solid foundation for your painting. You know exactly what you are going to paint and how you need to proceed.

As in any project you start, you need to have a plan and a sense of order. What style are you going to use? What is your subject matter going to be? Are you going to paint a landscape, a portrait or a still life? Before you start, you should make sure your canvas is well stretched and comfortably near you so you can easily work with it. Your tools, such as brushes and rags, should be placed within convenient reach and your palette established with the basic colors. You may wish to expand your palette as your painting takes form.

This is the first time we've mentioned the palette. For those of you who have never painted it is a board held by the artist that contains an array of colors to be used in the painting. Or, it can be the range and quality of colors on the board itself.

If the foundation isn't laid correctly your picture will lose some of its creativity. For instance, the composition will depend on how well you scale your picture to the size of canvas you've chosen. As with most construction projects if there is not careful preparation and a proper foundation there will be problems from the very beginning. If you try and continue without correcting the problem it will only get worse instead of better. However, if you've done all you know to do, and have prepared the foundation as instructed, your picture will turn out as planned.

The longer you contemplate and visualize the subject the more you can develop your imagination; this is where the creative process begins. After time and thought the artist is able to transfer his thoughts onto the canvas. The artist creates something that is beautiful and pleasing to look at. Concentration on the immediate visual impression is important. If I was to paint a picture and it appeared exactly as it looked, then I might as well have taken a picture.

If you are giving your own interpretation of a finished painting you may take some artistic liberties and add or delete a portion of the picture you want to change. For instance, if you are in a class and the instructor asks you to recreate a certain painting, and there are twenty students in the class, you will get twenty different interpretations of the same painting.

Early on when I became interested in painting, I did a portrait of an elderly woman. Before I started, I was looking at her and trying to imagine the finished picture. She had deep lines in her face and was quite large in stature not allowing me to imagine a very attractive finished portrait. I prayed, "Lord, let me capture her spirit and something memorable so she will like what I paint." As I looked more closely I saw a twinkle in her eye and a brightness I hadn't noticed before when just looking at her outward appearance. I focused on her inner beauty and the painting developed into a very nice piece that she truly loved.

Do you ever wonder what God was doing before the creation of the world? What was He thinking? I love to visualize Him planning the grass, the types of trees and each petal on every flower. I smile as I think of His ideas for the camels, elephants, giraffes and monkeys. This is how you should approach your painting, with careful planning, thoughtfulness and imagination.

During my early morning prayers I often reflect upon God and His creations and I get overwhelmed at the magnitude of who He is.

> *And God said, "Let us make man in our image, in our likeness; and let them have dominion over the fish of the sea, over the birds of the air, and over the livestock, and over all the earth, and over all the creatures that move upon the ground."*
> *So God created man in his own image, in the image of God he created him; male and female he created them. God blessed them and said to them, "Be fruitful and increase in number; fill the earth and subdue it. Rule over the fish of the sea and the birds of the air and over every living*

creature that moves on the ground.
Genesis 1:22-28.

Can you imagine the palette of colors God had to create such a universe? I sometimes try to think of the colors in heaven that we haven't seen here on earth. I'm sure our idea of Heaven is nothing compared to how it really is. God is waiting for every artist to discover the magnitude of colors available in His palette.

Now, as I sit contemplating, I try and reflect on what God was thinking when He made me. I am certain enough to think that what Psalm 139 says it must be true.

> *My frame was not hidden from you when I was being formed in secret [and] intricately and curiously wrought [as if embroidered with various colors] in the depths of the earth [a region of darkness and mystery]. Your eyes saw my unformed substance, and in your book all the days [of my life] were written before ever they took shape, when as yet there was none of them.*
> Psalms 139: 15-16. (AMP)

God's eyes saw my unformed substance and in His book all the days of my life were written when I was only a thought. Does that not seem like God's plan for my creation had a specific purpose? He was putting the charcoal to the canvas of my life way before I ever existed. I am humbled to think this means God had a plan for me and wanted me to accomplish something significant for His Kingdom.

God has plans for all of His children before we are born. He always has. The Bible gives us many examples going back to the beginning of time. Think of Abraham: here is what God said to Abraham:

> *Now [in Haran] the Lord said to Abraham, Go for yourself [for your own advantage] away from your country, from your relatives and your father's house, to the land that I will show you. And I will make you a great nation, and I will bless you [with abundant increase of favors] and make your name famous and distinguished, and you will be a blessing [dispensing good to other]."*
> Genesis 12:1

Abraham was living in a pagan country, doing well and God told him to leave his family, move to an unfamiliar place and He would bless him. Do you think he might have considered that to be an overwhelming request? Do you think he might have asked himself, "is this really God calling me?"

Abraham was seventy-five years old. Without hesitation he prepared his wife and nephew Lot, left his father's house and all that was familiar to him and did exactly what God asked him to do. Abraham's life had been carefully thought out. Everything was in place. Abraham did not know it at the time but God was providing him with the some of the final colors needed to finish his life portrait. God had a plan for Abraham long before he was born.

I would have asked a million questions and probably made some rather pointed remarks. First of all, I would have told God I was just too old to do what He was asking. If I had been Abraham I would have asked, "What if Sarah doesn't want to go? What will people think? What if I do go and fail?" However, Abraham became righteous because he believed. He used the colors God provided for his life canvas and finished his unique masterpiece. If we have faith, pray and search God out in the scriptures waiting patiently for His leading, we too can let God use the colors He has set aside for us to paint our portrait according to the outline already used for the foundation on our canvas.

Many times as we seek God we think we hear His voice, or find a scripture speaking directly to our needs, and then the old thoughts creep into our mind. Negativity or lack of faith takes over and we fail to respond to His call. But the call was there from the beginning. It was there when our canvas was blank and God was contemplating what colors to use and how to finish our masterpiece. If we allow God to be our foundation, the construction will stand firm.

When I was a young girl I had a lot of ideas of what I wanted to be when I grew up. However, my home environment was not affirming or one where I received much encouragement. My mother's only expectations were simply, graduate from high school, get a job and find a husband. So, I graduated from high school, got a job and found a husband. Not just any husband, the perfect husband. "Thank you Lord!"

My husband gave me all the affirmation I didn't get growing up. Every time I would share a dream or an idea with him he would encourage me to follow it through. He didn't try to discourage me or change my mind. Most importantly, he continually told me I could do anything I set my mind to.

Through the years I have been fortunate to have many people affirm me and encourage me to use my God given talents and abilities to further God's causes and spread the word of His love. God had a plan for my life. He directed me to my husband of 46 years, gave me the ability to speak and write, and He placed a fire inside of me to spread His word. Each step of the way He has directed me toward my destiny. Today I am an ordained minister and CEO of Generational Solutions, LLC. The company is a conglomerate, growing daily with God's leading. I've traveled around the world preaching His word and have lived a very full life.

The plan for my life work was planted within me from the beginning. God drew my outline providing a foundation for my life. Over the years a convergence of ideas, people, talents, and places came together to fulfill His plan for me.

Just as we start our paintings with an outline, faint at first but brought to fruition as we add layer upon layer of color and detail, so it is with our individual lives in God's hands as He paints our individual masterpieces. In my own life the outline was faint at first, without encouragement or direction, and yet as I worked with the handicapped, became an ordained minister, married and raised my children I listened for God's voice and followed His leading. My life is full. I'm doing what I love doing. Most importantly, I'm doing what I know God wants me to do. It is like this with all of us. Each person has a specific purpose, an assignment to be completed, and a canvas to be painted. If we don't follow the outline or listen carefully we won't be all that we can be.

I have a good friend who once told me that if I were to fail to do the work that I was created to do God would find someone else to do it. I have since found this to be a false statement. If it were true, the world would be a much better place.

Our creation was no accident; God had his plan right from the beginning. I shared this scripture in the first chapter but it would be good to reflect on it again in the Amplified Version.

> *For we are God's [own] handiwork [his workmanship], recreated in Christ Jesus, [born anew] that we may do those good works, which God predestined [planned beforehand] for us [taking paths which He prepared ahead of time], that we should walk in them [living the good life which He prearranged and made ready for us to live].*
> Ephesians 2:10 (AMP)

The construction has been laid, now it is time to add color.

Questions for Reflection

1) What does this Scripture tell me about God's plan for me?
2) When did God provide the outline for my life?
3) How do I know what specific assignment(s) God has for me?
4) Do I have the tools needed to finish my assignment?
5) Like Abraham, would I be willing to respond immediately to the call?

CHAPTER 4

YELLOW OCHRE
THE HOLY SPIRIT

~ *But when the Comforter (Counselor, Helper, Advocate, Intercessor, Strengthener, Standby) comes, whom I will send to you from the Father, the Spirit of Truth who comes (proceeds) from the Father, He (Himself) will testify regarding Me.* ~

John 15:26 (AMP)

Yellow Ochre is a color that blends in with all the other colors on a palette; it clarifies the color but does not destroy the purity of the color. It is applied after the charcoal construction is placed on the canvas. Unlike charcoal, which when placed too strongly on the canvas, will muddy a painting, Yellow Ochre allows the artist to see the definition of the painting.

When God gave me the outline for this book, He spoke to me saying, "As Yellow Ochre sets the definition for a painting, I assist all men and women in developing the purpose of their lives." God leads us but does not interfere. He gives us assistance through the Holy Spirit as we allow Him to enter our lives.

There was a time in my life when I was trying to find my way and I asked God about a specific thing I wanted to do. It wasn't a bad thing, however it was something that could have changed the direction of my life. God's answer was clear, "You can do anything you want, and you have free will." The choice was mine and the decision I made had to be my decision. God knew if I made the decision on my own and it didn't turn out well I couldn't blame Him for the outcome.

Choice has a lot to do with the outcome of our lives. I realized the Holy Spirit was waiting for me to respond to Him. During those early years of my life, He was patient with me. He would gently lead me as I made decisions and opened doors that led me in the right direction. It was up to me to listen to my conscience and once the door was opened, make the decision to go through it.

Years ago while meditating, I had an experience I have never forgotten. There was music playing in the background and subconsciously I began to follow the notes. The next thing I remember I felt as if I were going through a waterfall and coming out into a dark cave. Bats were flying all around my head and I was walking on a paved road that had rocks and boulders all along the way. I had to step over and around each obstacle while swatting the bats from around my head at the same time. I had a sense that the bats represented turmoil and the stones and boulders were obstacles that I would have to overcome in the journey of my life as the Holy Spirit led me to my destiny. Interestingly enough, the road under my feet was paved. It was as though the Holy Spirit was laying the foundation for my journey so I wouldn't become discouraged if I encountered obstacles along life's way.

The Holy Spirit is our support system. He is with us always.

> *However, I am telling you nothing but the truth when I say it is profitable (good expedient, advantageous) for you that I go away. Because if I do not go away, the Comforter (Counselor, Helper, Advocate, Intercessor, Strengthener, Standby) will not come to you ((into close fellowship with you) but if I go away, I will send Him to you (to be in close fellowship with you).*
> John 16:7 (AMP)

Advocate, comforter, counselor, helper, intercessor, standby, strengthener, these are all adjectives that describe the Holy Spirit. He's there for us whenever we need Him.

> *Everything that the Father has is mine. That is what I meant when I said that He (the Spirit) would take the things that are*

mine and will reveal (declare, disclose, transmit) it to you.
John 16:15 (AMP)

The Holy Spirit will reveal to us all we need to know. The Greek translation for reveal is "anggello," which means declaration. The Holy Spirit is declaring over our lives a purpose and destiny that will lead us into a place of self-actualization, i.e., living out our full potential.

Just as the Yellow Ochre sets the charcoal on our painting for a stronger foundation to follow, the Holy Spirit wants us to listen carefully for His leading so we can discover our true purpose in life. Remember, He has pre-ordained us long before we were born, with a plan. However, it is up to us to choose to listen, and allow Him to lead and before we can truly find our destiny.

> *For I know the thoughts and plans that I have for you, says the Lord, thoughts and plans for welfare and peace and not for evil, to give you hope in your final outcome. Then you will call upon Me, and you will come and pray to Me, and I will hear and heed you. Then you will seek Me, inquire for, and require Me (as a vital necessity) and find Me when you search for Me with all your heart.*
> Jeremiah 29:11-13 (AMP)

Applying the Yellow Ochre is a quick process because the faint lines of the charcoal have already been put onto canvas. The Yellow Ochre is there to add definition to the images, thus making it easier for the next step.

That's the way it is with the Holy Spirit. The foundation of our life has already been put into place. The Holy Spirit makes it easier for us to follow through on each project, job and ministry involvement that we might have. He is there ever-present knowing just what we need, when we need it and leading us through the process. He wants to be involved and He wants to help.

I've discovered over the years that with each new project in my life I must take time to invite God into the process. I want the Holy Spirit to assist me in everything I do. I heard an acquaintance and marketplace minister once say, "Every revelation from God will be manifested in the natural."

My personal experience has been that I can't always depend on the supernatural experience to bring me into a deeper relationship with God. Please hear me out on this. I don't discount the supernatural experience. However, I don't have to have that kind of an experience to mature in my relationship with God.

As I travel and participate in my ministry I meet many people who are anxious to get the next prophetic word or have a supernatural experience so they will know God is working in their life and they can make a decision to move forward with their life. God has already given us a path and an assistant in the Holy Spirit to lead us. We don't have to have God sit us down and spell it out for us. He gave us our mind, an intelligent mind. If we pray and listen to our conscious, the Holy Spirit will lead us as we make all the decisions in our life. John 16 says: **"Everything the Father has is mine."** Through Jesus we can have it all too. The Holy Spirit will declare it over us.

When I first start a painting, as the artist, I have to decide what I want to paint. Am I going to paint a still life or a landscape? Whichever I decide on, the ability to create that painting is already within.

So many of us are afraid to take a deeper look into who and what we really are. We struggle trying to find our niche in life when it is already there. What if you always like to help out in the kitchen cooking, but your dad said you should be a dentist, like him. You were miserable thinking about looking into people's mouths all day, but thought you would be a failure if you didn't go into dentistry like your dad. Then one summer you helped cook at your church's retreat and were told you were wonderful at it. You were organized, had good menus and the food was delicious. Think God might have had a different path in mind for you? Just maybe you are meant to be a Chef. If we take the initiative and look closely we realize God has given us all we need to be successful. The joy of that discovery in God's love is amazing!

What if Mary hadn't responded to the angel when he told her she was to be the mother of the Savior? What if she had said, "Not me, I'm not going to carry that child. I'm a virgin. You know what people will say and what might happen to me or my family." Not to mention the fact that she could have faced death by stoning. However, Mary did heed the call of the Holy Spirit and by so doing she fulfilled her purpose in life.

Within all of us lies abilities, desires, dreams, God given talents and the passion to do something amazing for the Kingdom. We just have to stay true to our calling and listen for God's leading.

People have often asked me, "How do you know the call of God in your life?" First of all, we have to be comfortable with our own skin, our own talents and the gifts God gave us. Many people spend too much time looking at other people's lives, wanting to be as successful, or look like they do. Sometimes they desire to be someone else so much that they neglect to realize they have their own set of talents and success within them just waiting to be discovered. If you don't look within you won't see the beauty of who you are.

> *The watchman opens the door for this man, and the sheep listen to his voice and*

heed it; and he calls his own sheep by name and brings (leads) them out. When he has brought his own sheep outside he walks on before them, and the sheep follow him because they know his voice.
John: 10:3-4.

Many times in life people fail simply because they can't believe they are worthy of success. "God use me? I don't think so." Some people actually believe if they enjoy what they are doing it must be wrong. After all, aren't we supposed to have to sacrifice for the glory of God? How sad some people can't accept the gifts they have been given and listen to the Holy Spirit to utilize them for His glory. David was a shepherd, but became a king. Joseph was traded by his brothers as a boy and grew up to save Israel from famine. Mary was a quiet girl living with her family when she was chosen to give birth to the Christ Child. Every one of us has a job to do for the Kingdom. It may not look like we have the qualifications, but God will make sure we find our purpose if we listen to the Holy Spirit and follow His leading.

Jesus said: "For this reason I am telling you, whatever you ask for in prayer, believe (trust and be confident) that it is granted to you, and you will (get it)
Mark 11:24.

To not believe what Jesus said would take away any credibility from His word.

The Holy Spirit assists in our accomplishing our life path set before us just as the Yellow Ochre blends the outline for our painting and prepares the way for the next step to our masterpiece.

Questions for Reflection

1) Can you think of a specific incident where the Holy Spirit led you to make a decision that changed your life?
2) Are you able to accept that you do have a purpose to fulfill for the kingdom and the Holy Spirit will lead you to that purpose if you listen carefully for His leading?

CHAPTER 5

TONING

COMING FROM THE DARK TO LIGHT

~ Your eye is the lamp of your body, when your eye (your conscience) is sound and fulfilling its office, your whole body is full of light; but when it is not sound and is not fulfilling its office, your body is full of darkness. Be careful, therefore, that the light that is in you is not darkness. If then your entire body is illuminated, having no part dark, it will be wholly bright (with light), as when a lamp with its bright rays gives you light. ~

Luke 11:34-36 (AMP)

Toning is the next step in Impressionistic painting. Looking at your subject, squinting, you look for the darkest dark, painting from that point toward the light. Using the side of your brush, you paint lightly by rubbing the paint onto the canvas. Squinting is an important part of the process. The more you squint, the more you see the dark places. It is interesting to note, that when you squint, what would not normally seem dark becomes dark. As you begin to fill in the canvas, you visualize the final painting. When you look at the painting you should get the sense of walking into it the scene. If you are painting a landscape for example, you should be able to follow a path leading you to an imaginary spot. If you paint too dark on certain spots, you will create a picture that is unbalanced. Your eye will be drawn to the mistake rather than the entire canvas. It's the same with us. If there are any personal constraints within us, they will become apparent just as the darkness appears on the canvass, and people will begin to see what we don't want them to see.

There was a time in my life when I was extremely angry. The loss of relationships, job and ministry all contributed to my anger. I thought my anger was justified in some part, but it didn't excuse my anger. The anger interfered with every part of my being. It affected not only my behavior, but also my health, and it spilled over into everyone I came into contact with. Making matters worse, I couldn't see my own condition. I had hidden emotional pain so deep within me my entire life was out of control. Although I thought I was okay, I was not. What I was projecting to people wasn't the love of God but the pain that came from within. Fortunately, with help, I took responsibility for my actions and dealt with the issues that had caused my pain. It was a difficult process and took a long time.

Coming out of darkness into the light isn't always easy, but it is certainly worth the journey. Allowing the Holy Spirit to speak to our heart, and heal our wounds, and asking Him for guidance will bring the peace we need. Trusting God every day to keep us in His care and help us walk in the light of His holiness will bring us the peace that surpasses all understanding. The Holy Spirit can reach the deepest, darkness of our souls and gently pull us to the light just as the painter starts in the darkest of dark and paints outward to the light.

What causes a person to live in darkness? The answer is different for each person. Everyone has experienced hurts and failures that have caused reactions, and if not dealt with, can lead to unresolved conflicts. However, God can and will change us if we ask. If we don't seek help, our emotions will become confused and life will become a struggle. Decision we make will be made for the wrong reasons, possibly leading us off the path of our destiny. It will be difficult to hear the Holy Spirit clearly speaking to us and leading us in our daily life.

Recently I asked God, "What causes a person who knows the truth and lived the truth to turn away from all they know to be good and righteous?

God spoke to me in a clear voice. "The enemy is insidious. He works on us little by little. He finds cracks in our spiritual armor and works on that small opening until it becomes a fracture."

For instance, let's say your home is important to you. You worked hard for it, you've lived there many years, raised your children, had a dog, buried the dog in the yard when it died, you know, all the things that make a house a home. Suddenly and very unexpectedly you lose your job. In today's economy this could be a reality. Circumstances prevent you from making payments, and desperation sets in. That house with all the memories and safety it has provided for you through the years is now in foreclosure. You cry out to God, "Where are you, why don't you help me." Worrying about your home may be a crack in your armor but when worry becomes despair it is a fracture. But, God will help as we allow the circumstances of life paint color on our canvas. Rather than doing all we can do and trusting God, we give up. Not only do we give up we blame God for our circumstances. In the ignorance of our shortsightedness we walk away. The darkness covers us like a heavy, black cloud. And, our relationship with God has changed.

Maybe the deception is much cagier than that. Maybe it starts as a drink with a friend at a club after work. You were never really into alcohol but it taste good and you love the social aspect of going somewhere after work. It starts with one drink, becomes two and maybe even three. You drink every evening, you drink on the weekend, you buy liquor for home; before you know it you're an alcoholic! It starts to affect your work. First you're late, then you call in sick because you drank too much the night before and have a hangover. When you do work you don't do your work well. Before long your boss calls you in and wants to know what's happening with you? It's not my fault! At least that's what you tell yourself.

Obviously, the causes for alcoholism are much greater than just starting to drink with a friend after work, at least we hope so, but you get the picture. We think we are invincible and nothing can happen that would cause us to stray away from God. However, it does happen.

Satan is sly, deceitful and full of tricks. He finds where he can hit us in our weakness and goes for our hearts. Our heart becomes hardened and we fall into his trap. We stopped listening to the Holy Spirit. We've been deceived. God cannot draw us toward the light (Him) if we turn our backs on Him.

It is important to note that without darkness there can be no light. And, the darkness vanishes only when we turn toward the light. When painting, you can't have a painting with all light, that would be impossible, just as it would be impossible to have a painting that was all dark. Even if you used the same color for the entire painting, you would have to use different shades or degrees of the color to make the painting come alive.

While writing parts of this book I am in Cape Porpoise, Maine. It is beautiful here and very quiet. I'm sitting at looking out the window of a converted barn overlooking a lobster-fishing village. The beauty of the boats in the harbor, the blue water, islands off in the distance and the lighthouse will make for a quintessential view of New England. I often take my paints and easel with me when I travel to Maine knowing there will be an abundance of beautiful scenes to paint.

Today I thought it would be nice to paint a landscape. As I survey my supplies, I realize I've forgotten my paint box with all of my brushes, pallet and even some of my paint. I'm disappointed but it's really no problem. This town is full of artists and art supply stores, so I know I'm going shopping.

The art store is close by and seems to have everything I need. I don't want to spend a lot of money so I purchase mostly disposable items. Remembering I have some paints with me I decide I have just enough to do the job.

Here's my problem. I decided I wanted to finish a painting I had started a year ago. I had already done some of the toning. However, now it was a different time of the year. The new season would require different colors. Because I had left my paints at home I didn't have many colors to choose from. I was forced to practice mixing the colors I had. I would be painting a fall scene rather than the summer scene I had originally started with. I decided to accomplish the needed changes I would need to do some heavy toning. Needless to say, I created a bit of a mess on my canvas. Now I had to make the choice of either letting the canvas dry and fix my mistakes or start over with a new canvas. I decided I would correct my mistakes.

We are faced with choices every day of our lives. If we are not careful and keep a watchful eye, darkness can overcome us very unexpectedly. The Bible says to pray without ceasing. Now, that doesn't mean we need to be on our knees all the time. However, we can become so aware of God in our life that we are in constant communication with Him as we walk throughout our day. It is so much easier to keep in touch with God on a daily basis and live in His light than to get lost in the darkness. God is always present. He knows what's happening in our lives every minute of every day.

> *If I say, "Surely the darkness shall fall on me. Even the night shall be [the only] light about me; Even, the darkness hides nothing from You, but the night shines as the day; the darkness and the light are both alike to you."*
> Psalm 139:11-12 (AMP)

This area of Maine is very quiet this time of year. I'm not used to quiet. If I am guilty of anything, it is being too busy. I am a task-oriented person, always doing something or wanting to start something. I am a forerunner, a networker and a leader. I teach and travel and am very involved in our family businesses, yes businesses. I tend to be unable to be quiet for very long. I love being around people. Coming to Maine was a huge step for me.

I've wanted to write this book for some time. It's very important to me. I knew if I did not take the time out and find a quiet place to devote just to my writing it would never happen.

When I am alone with God, I discover who I really am. I find out my weaknesses, strengths and my constraints. And in this quiet place I become aware of the dark places in my soul.

> *Yet to us God has unveiled and revealed them by and through His Spirit, for the [Holy] Spirit searches diligently, exploring and examining everything, even sounding the profound and bottomless things of God [the divine counsels and things hidden and beyond man's scrutiny].*
> 1 Cor. 2:10 (AMP)

We all have areas of our lives that need tending too. Some of our personal constraints (or dark areas if you will) are darker than others. Only the Holy Spirit can reveal to us what areas we need to work on. Just as the artist examines his painting for areas to improve, God examines our hearts and minds and continues to lead us to the light through the Holy Spirit.

> *Search me, O God, and know my heart; try me, and know my anxieties; and see if*

there is any wicked way I me, and lead me
in the way everlasting.
Psalm 139: 23-24. (NKJV)

When we learn to dwell in the light, God can lead us to the next level of our lives. He adds color to our canvas and takes us a step closer to finishing our masterpiece.

The toning process fills the whole canvas with color, leaving the lightest light blank. You never put in the lightest light until you are ready to complete the canvas. It is that way with us. When we receive Christ as our Savior, we are saved. The Greek word for salvation is sozo, which means we are healed and being healed. It is an ongoing process. Occasionally when I make a really big mistake on one of my paintings, as I did with the one I am working on now, I take turpentine and rub away the area where the mistake was made and start the process over.

> *The Lord is merciful and gracious, slow to anger and plenteous in mercy and loving-kindness.*
> *He will not always chide or be contending, neither will he keep His anger forever or hold a grudge.*
> *He has not dealt with us after our sins nor rewarded us according to our iniquities for the heavens are high above the earth, so great are His mercy and*

loving-kindness   toward   those   who
reverently and worshipfully fear Him.
As far as the east is from the west, so far
has He removed our transgressions from
us!
Psalm 103: 8-12 (AMP)

When we make right choices, allowing God to work in our life, repenting and accepting the changes He gives us, He wipes all of our sins away, remembering them no more. Instead of using turpentine, He uses His love to bring healing to correct our mistakes.

By the time we start applying the toning on the canvas we should have a good idea of where we are headed. If we start with the end in mind, we remain focused so when we make mistakes we can confidently correct them. So it is with our lives.

Toning is miraculous. During this process we will begin to see everything come together on the canvas. There have been times when I was almost complete with the toning and realized I didn't like what I was seeing. I want to give up and start over. I've learned, through trial and error, that when I persevere and keep working on what has been done, my mistakes, when corrected, can actually add value, and beauty, and then I am satisfied with the results. The biggest mistake we can make when painting, and in our lives, is to believe we are not capable of making the necessary changes and finishing the masterpiece planned from the beginning. We all make mistakes. But when we keep working to correct our mistakes and trust God, things will work out according to His plan.

Have you ever noticed there didn't seem to be anyone with noticeable qualifications to fulfill the tasks God assigned them. Abraham was too old to father a child, a child that had his own destiny to fulfill for God. However because of his faith in God Abraham did what God asked him to do without hesitation or question.

Consider David. David was a shepherd. He spent most of his young life tending his flock. He was simply delivering lunch to his brothers when he encountered the giant, Goliath of Gath. Goliath was ten feet tall and, his armor weighed 5000 shekels of bronze. The only experience David had in fighting was when he saved the sheep in his care from a lion and later a bear. However, there he stood and something deep inside him told him he would kill the giant. The Holy Spirit was talking to David leading him to his destiny. You know the story. David killed the giant! With a smooth stone and a slingshot! God had a plan for David's life. The giant was just the beginning.

For David to kill the giant, he had to live in the present and the presence of God. He knew he was supposed to kill that giant. When all that emotion rose up in him and he heard the giant mock the

The Blank Canvas

living God, he was ready to do battle. This is what I call a convergence experience. A convergence is when an event in life shows themes that will evolve into a life purpose. By killing the giant David began the journey to the rest of his life's purpose. After killing Goliath, David had favor with the king and everyone realized David was more than just a shepherd.

Just as it took faith for David to step forward and kill the giant, it takes faith to put the dark paint on the canvas when beginning a painting. It looks odd when you first start, but as it blends in you can see there is a purpose for this step and it does in fact make way for the rest of the painting.

Everyone has a purpose in life. I mentioned my daughter Gretchen earlier. She was a delight. Everyone that met her could feel the love she had inside her. If Gretchen was sitting on the sofa and someone came to visit she always wanted to give him or her a hug. The visitor would need to sit down of course to get the hug and they would always give one in return. This was no ordinary hug. This was a hug that was full of genuine love. When she finished with what she thought was the appropriate hug, time wise, she would gently rest her head on their chest and remain quiet and content until the visitor prepared to leave.

Compared to the standard the world appears to be setting forth today, a person with Gretchen's disabilities would be considered a hindrance rather than a blessing. She didn't see, she didn't speak, and was severely physically and mentally handicapped. Her parents rejected her. The doctors said she would give up her will to live, and she would have no purpose in her life. They said she wouldn't live past the age of three. They were wrong. Gretchen did have a purpose. She gave unconditional love to everyone she met. She taught patience, love and devotion to everyone who came to know her. God had a plan for Gretchen's life and she fulfilled it every day of her 27 years on earth.

Finding our purpose is a process. During the process we grow and mature in our relationship with Christ. It is in the difficult times, when we feel we are totally in darkness, and afraid to look for the light that we learn to listen for God. It's easy to look back and see what we didn't accomplish. But even those times helped us grow closer to God.

Having goals in life is a good thing. As we walk work toward our goals it might be easy to rush through the process. Taking each step, being patient and not rushing will help us achieve what we are after. This is hard for me. I often rush into things thinking it is a good idea. However, before long I realize my life is pretty muddy and I don't have a clear path to where I'm going. I have to stay in the present when working on a project. Yesterday is gone and the future isn't here yet. Each day I must work for that day to do what is necessary to reach my goal. Once again, it is the same when doing a painting. We cannot rush. We complete each phase to prepare for the next step. Each step leads us to the finished masterpiece we are painting.

Recently after reading a devotional my husband shared a new revelation with me, "resurrection rest brings resurrection power!" When we rest in the Father's love, we receive power and direction to move forward to our destiny.

> *We are assured and know that [God being a partner in their labor] all things work together and are [fitting into a plan] for good to and for those who love God and are called according to [His] design and purpose.*
> Romans 8:28 (AMP)

God was with Abraham and David. He is also with you and me. My life hasn't always been easy. Growing up in a dysfunctional family, I experienced abuse, illness and poverty. I've experienced the loss of a child, had numerous surgeries, including having my colon removed and a liver transplant. Long before they tested blood for HIV, I had 185 blood transfusions. Looking at the medical procedures alone, I should not be alive.

On a more positive note, I have wonderful husband and we have been married for 46 years. We have three natural children and two adopted children. I was ordained into the ministry in 1988. Since being ordained it has been my privilege to serve on numerous boards, international ministries and prayer organizations. I've been a Pastor, started several non-profit organizations, and became a life coach/master life strategist. I've been involved in most of the Seven Mountains of Influence, arts and entertainment, business, education, family, government and religion.

Throughout my life I have had to work to bring my character flaws in order and ask God for guidance so I could excel in any one of these areas. I couldn't dwell on my past mistakes and move forward at the same time. We all have things in our past that, if we dwell on them, would make us feel we couldn't possibly be chosen by God for a special purpose. This is a lie literally from the pit of hell, trying to discourage us and keep us from attaining our goal. We must look for the light and not dwell in the dark.

The toning process puts substance on the canvas. It is the last step in our painting before putting on the pure color. The Holy Spirit has reached deep into our darkest secrets and led us to the light. For some, finding our purpose seems easy. For others it appears in the process of growing in Christ. We are now ready to apply pure color to our canvas and complete our masterpiece.

Questions for Reflection

1. Am I holding onto something dark that keeps me from discovering my true purpose for my life?
2. Has the Holy Spirit tried to lead me to my true path and I've ignored Him?

CHAPTER 6

CROSS HATCHING
APPLYING PURE COLOR

~ Come to Me, all you who labor and are heavy-laden and overburdened, and I will cause you to rest. (I will ease and relieve and refresh your souls.) ~

Matthew 11:28 (AMP)

Cross-hatching is just what it says—you apply paint to the canvas in the form of a cross. Again going from the dark to light, you apply pure color with this repeated motion. My teacher was adamant about both the technique and using pure color. She would scold us if she saw us using any solution that might dilute the pure color of the oil paint. As the painting develops, you begin to see the beauty of the creation process. Color begins to explode all over the canvas and everything flows together to make a remarkable picture. This is the final step to complete our masterpiece.

Cross-hatching is an important process in Impressionistic painting. But how does this technique apply to our lives? The answer to this question is: look to Jesus, and consider God's gift at the cross. He is the author and perfector of our faith.

*Looking away [from all that will distract]
to Jesus, who is the leader and source of
our faith [giving the first incentive for
our belief] and is also its finisher
[bringing it to maturity and perfection].
He, for the joy [of obtaining the prize]
that was set before Him, endured the
cross.*
Hebrews 12:2 (AMP)

Jesus set the standard. I think we can all agree He is a masterpiece. The purpose of His earthy life was established long before that starry night in Bethlehem. I'm sure God the Father created the outline with Jesus, before the creation of the world, so there would be no misunderstanding for the purpose of His incarnation.

God the Father chose Joseph and Mary to assist in the plan as earthly parents for Jesus, and the Holy Spirit to lead Him through His good times and His bad times here on earth. Scripture tells us that Jesus wasn't necessarily an attractive man. However, as He walked the earth people were drawn to Him as He taught, healed the sick and fed the multitude, Meanwhile, He was preparing for the next chapter of His life.

What if you knew that you were going to be betrayed by someone you loved? Can you imagine the pain that pierced Christ's heart when Judas kissed him on the cheek? Can you imagine praying in Gethsemane, hearing the soldiers advancing and knowing what was coming for you knowing what was inevitable?

"Change of plans Father, I want out," would have been my words.

Trials and tribulations: I don't much care for those words. Yet, if we've lived at all, we've had both trials and tribulations. As painful as they may be, if we trust God, and persevere, we will grow in His love.

As the time came closer it appeared Jesus didn't want to go to the cross. Here was His prayer:

> *My soul is overwhelmed with sorrow to the point of death. Stay here and keep watch with me." Going a little farther, He fell with His face to the ground and prayed, "My father, if it is possible, may this cup be taken from me. Yet not as I will, but as you will.*
> Matthew 26:38-39.

Later in Hebrew 12:2 we are told He went for the joy of obtaining the prize that was set before Him. You and I are that prize. Because of what Jesus did on the cross, we live not only for eternity, but so our life here on earth can be fulfilled. This doesn't mean we won't have trials and tribulations, but as we embrace the cross, surrender our lives to Christ and live daily in Him, we will walk in His light, receive His blessings and provide Him with another stroke of pure color for our canvas.

Our personalities reflect God's personal gifts to us. When we recognize this and utilize our gifts to His purpose, we grow in God's love. Our character reflects the character of Christ. That means no dull colors!

When each step of our purpose on earth is met as laid out by our Father before we were born, our pure colors will be bright and not diluted.

I worked for a Christian counseling agency for a period of time. Often the discussion would come up about the need to embrace the crosses in our lives. In all my years as a Christian, I had never heard this terminology and was a bit surprised by the phrase.

My assumption was always that Jesus endured the cross, so why would I have to? Doesn't scripture say that by the stripes we are healed? I guess I thought maybe I had a free ride. I learned a good lesson. As I grew in Christ I learned to confront my problems instead of running away from them. I took full responsibility for them and did whatever I could do to correct the situation. I would surrender and ask God, "What am I to learn from this Father?"

This surrender didn't come easy. But the longer I tried to fix my own problems, the longer the problems would last. Now as situations arise in my life I often get a little excited, I know God will see me through it. He is at work in my life. I can now say I use each situation as an opportunity for growth in my walk with God. Instead of reacting to what comes my way I try and respond accordingly and look the situation at hand straight on. This process has made a great difference in my day-to-day life.

Easter of 2009 our family went through a particularly hard time. Our son Paul and his family came home for the Holiday, which was always exciting. There was lots of activity in the house, laughter, talking and everyone telling their latest news. As a mother, I relished these times.

On Sunday morning there was the bustling of everyone getting ready for church, eating breakfast and getting out the door on time. When we arrived home there was more activity as we began to get lunch on the table. My husband decided to sit on the sofa with our daughter Gretchen until we were ready to eat. She was now 27 years old. As I told you before her young body had battled blindness, cerebral palsy, a seizure disorder and severe mental incapability's along with many complications that go along with any of the above-mentioned physical problems her entire life. None of her problems kept her from being one of the most delightful people I have ever known.

As I mentioned earlier, when Gretchen met someone she never forgot who he or she were. With all of her disabilities she extended love to everyone she met. She would become quite indignant if after she met someone they forgot to come over and say hello on any visit after their first encounter. When you asked her where Jesus lived, she would point to her heart.

I was scurrying about trying to get dinner on the table when I walked by where Gretchen and my husband were sitting and suddenly noticed she was very pale and beginning to turn blue. Without hesitation I dialed 911. My son Paul and daughter Tracy applied CPR. Their quick thinking actually saved her life. An undisclosed illness had created serious symptoms and we would soon discover this was only the first of many visits to the emergency room in an attempt to save her young life.

After three months of scary moments and more ER visits than I care to remember, believing it was time, we made the painful decision to take our sweet Gretchen off of life-support allowing her to go home to be with the Lord.

As handicapped as Gretchen was we still asked the questions that families ask when they lose a loved one. Why did she have to die so young? Why wasn't she healed? Those questions will be with us until we see God and He shares the answers with us. I know this. She was a very personal gift to me from

Him. She gave me unconditional love. She taught me patience and I would affirm her every day. One day in particular she was acting out. It was almost impossible to discover the root of Gretchen's discomfort. Because she couldn't communicate verbally, we had to rely on her pointing to her pain and wait it out. This day I couldn't seem to find the source of her frustration. I had worked with her for quite awhile cleaning her, bathing her and getting her dressed. That in itself could often times be an ordeal. She began to fight me. When that didn't work she became self-abusive. (This often happens with severely handicapped people) I simply did not know how to help her. Out of my own frustration I began to cry and pray out loud. When Gretchen heard me she immediately stopped and reached out for a hug. It was an amazing time. It was as if God was hugging me Himself.

I have never loved anyone the way I loved Gretchen. At the time of the writing of this book she has been gone for two years and yet the pain in my heart is as if it were yesterday. There is a void in my life no one can ever fill. However, I must tell you, Gretchen provided such vibrant colors in my life and in turn allowed me to grow in God and add pure color to my own canvas that I wouldn't exchange my time with her for anything. Gretchen was part of my life journey. She was part of the pure color God used when applying the cross hatching to my masterpiece.

Weeping may endure for a night, but joy
comes in the morning.
Psalms 30:5 (AMP)

When we learn to embrace the pain we are confronted with in our lives and walk through it with God we become equipped to comfort others in their time of sorrow.

> *Blessed be the God and Father of our Lord*
> *Jesus Christ, the Father of sympathy (pity*
> *and mercy) and the God [Who is the*
> *Source] of every comfort [consolation and*
> *encouragement]. Who comforts [consoles*
> *and encourages] us in every trouble*
> *calamity and affliction], so that we may*
> *also be able to comfort [console and*
> *encourage] those who are in any kind of*
> *trouble or distress, with the comfort*
> *[consolation and encouragement [with*
> *which we ourselves are comforted*
> *[consoled and encouraged] by God.*
> 2 Corinthians 1: 3-4. (AMP)

Let's look at this scripture. Our heavenly Father is sympathetic, has pity and mercy, and is the source of every comfort. As we seek Him, He will comfort us in every trouble. The scripture doesn't indicate that we should turn and run away from our trouble. It says that He is the source of our comfort.

We must look at each relationship, each event and each decision in our lives as a lesson to be learned. We must listen for the leading of the Holy Spirit and move forward trusting.

Let's not get burdened down with thinking our lives will be all pain and sorrow. Or, that God causes the pain and suffering in our lives. We live in a broken world. The enemy is running to and fro trying his best to deceive us. God allows these problems in our life but assures us He will never allow anything we cannot handle. If He didn't allow the pain we would never know of His love. Or, for that fact, we would never have to make choices to trust God and serve Him. There would be no free will. All of our choices would be made for us.

God gives us many wonderful gifts to rejoice in! All good gifts come from God. When we do receive favor or gifts from God it is not so we can brag to others or run around and be pious. It is so we can help others on their life journey. As we live in God's light we become an example to others.

Remember the song, "Everybody Needs Somebody Sometime?" When Gretchen passed away we had many, many friends that came to pay their respects and give their support of love. It was very gratifying to know Gretchen had touched so many lives and we had so many friends. My husband and I have a strong relationship with each other and with God. We trust Him in all ways. However, we were hurting. We needed someone to lean on. We needed human contact and comfort. Fortunately, we had wonderful Christian friends that stayed with us and did just that. They were people who had received love and support during difficult times in their lives and were able to pass it on to others.

We can experience joy when we use the experiences we have to bring comfort to others in their time of sorrow. Nothing is lost when we allow God to take our pain, teach us to grow from it and pass on healing to others. Pain is not easy. But we cannot dwell on the pain. Don't look back, we have to continue to look to God and move forward with our lives.

We want all the colors on our canvas to be pure color not diluted. We want our lives to reflect God's love for mankind. We want bright, pure colors in our masterpiece. All the experiences of life add that color to our canvas.

Questions for Reflections

1. What experiences have you had that allowed you to grow and mature in your relationship with God, allowing Him to put pure color on our canvas?

2. Have you been honest with God and spoken to Him about areas of hurt in your life that you know you are holding onto?

CHAPTER 7

THE COMPLETE MASTERPIECE

~ What lies behind us and what lies before us are tiny matters compared to what lies within us. ~

Walt Emerson

You are a masterpiece waiting to emerge!

Coming to the end of the painting and applying the pure color is very exciting. You see the objects in your painting taking form and the light and dark colors coming together balancing the picture on the canvas. The painting is even and well suited to the canvas. One part of the painting should not stand out more than the other. You should be able to see the whole picture, and the paint should be evenly distributed across the canvas.

Several years ago I took a week long intensive painting class. For eight hours a day I observed an experienced artist demonstrating the various techniques and learning some of the very things I have explained to you in earlier pages of this book. Of course, the instruction and demonstration was for the benefit of myself and other members of the class, as we would soon begin our own painting. There were a number of subjects we could choose from for our painting. I chose to do a portrait.

The young lady to be the model for the portrait was quite beautiful. She had dark hair and a very light complexion. (I need to make a small diversion here and let you know that painting a portrait was somewhat intimidating to me.) However, I wanted to push myself and do it anyway.

Wanting to do well with my chosen subject I was very careful as I began and wanted to apply the paint to my canvas as close to the teacher's instruction as possible.

As my art teacher approached my canvas to critique my work I was very nervous. He stood back and observed, moved closer to study the canvas, looked at the young lady posing as my model and then glanced at me. Imagine my shock when he immediately mixed colors on my pallet and painted black paint all over the right side of my portrait. Until that very moment, I actually thought I had been doing a good job. However, the look on his face as he said, "fix it," indicated I might have overestimated myself. All the insecurities that I thought I had hidden deep within me for years, rose up and I could feel panic approaching. My thoughts seemed to be screaming, "you can't fix this. You're not a real artist!"

Taking a deep breath and standing back for a few minutes I managed to direct my thoughts to my, "I can do it," mode and moved forward. Portrait painting is not easy, especially for a beginner like me with limited abilities. However, it was something I was very determined to do. I carefully reviewed the entire canvas. I saw areas that could use improvement and identified mistakes where the teacher had concerns. I knew instinctively if I were to become a good artist I had to put my emotions aside and move forward with the portrait before me.

The instructor for my class certainly wasn't liked much among the students. He could, at times, be what some would call rude and very direct. But I came to realize he was full of passion for the art of painting and wanted his students to truly learn how to paint. It was true, on the surface my class appeared to be not much more than a group of older women who possibly had nothing more to do than spend time looking for classes to take. But the instructor knew that somewhere in that class there were one or two people that truly wanted to become artist and hidden inside of them was raw talent waiting to be awakened. His method may not have been applauded but his purpose was clear.

Although the portrait isn't the best work I have done I keep it hung in a prominent place in my living room to remind me of that early lesson learned: Mistakes are sometimes necessary. This is true in painting as well as in life. Without mistakes we would not earn the right way of painting a beautiful portrait or come out of the shadows of our life and see the light of God.

God often uses the same process in our lives when trying to help us discover our true path. He sees our mistakes, usually made because we haven't listened to the Holy Spirit or followed His leading. He covers our mistakes and gently says, "do it over, this time listen carefully to My instruction."

Remember, God doesn't cause the hardships we encounter; we are often responsible for them ourselves. We also like to say, "the devil made me do it." Again, that's not always true. Although, we have an enemy who works against us, we often cause our own problems. Satan knows our weaknesses and will put in a little lie that will make us wander down a track that goes nowhere. Even though God allows these trials to enter our lives, He never leaves us while we encounter them and He is always ready to help us through them. All we have to do is call upon Him for His guidance.

Not long ago I was having lunch with a friend who was going through some very difficult times in her life. I listened carefully as she expressed doubt, fear and guilt—a bad combination for anyone going through hardships. When she was finished telling me all she was experiencing I began to share with her some of my past experiences and how God had led me through each one. She was surprised and amazed as I told her of my illnesses and near death experiences, my many surgeries and the loss of my daughter. She was astounded that I had such a positive attitude and was still so anxious to tell of God's love. The old hymn, <u>Lean On Me</u>, probably says it best. That's exactly what I have learned to do. God always sees us through our difficult times if we just lean on Him. And each time we lean on Him we add pure color to our canvas.

Whenever I do something creative and come to the end of the project it is a bittersweet time. My desire to see the finished work and the anticipation is very exciting. However, there is always the fear that no one will like it. My teacher taught the class that we should never call ourselves anything less than an artist. As I would look around during those lessons I would often compare my work with others in the class. I'm a very practical person. I could see that there were others doing better work than mine. There were some I was a little envious of; I wished I could paint as well as they did. And there were others, in my opinion that just were not as good as I was. But I decided to call myself an artist no matter how good or bad I thought I was, to have the attitude I was a good artist, not being proud or boastful, but confident and to be the very best artist I could with the talent I had been given. I learned not to compare myself with others. I realized each artist has his or her own style and each piece is a reflection of that particular artist. There really isn't a bad painting. There are just paintings that reflect different styles of different artists. Each person paints their own masterpiece in their own style just as God paints each of our lives to reflect the masterpiece He means for us to be.

The Song of Solomon expresses the love for the Father beautifully in the follow passage:

> You are beautiful, my darling, as Tirzah, lovely as Jerusalem, majestic as troops with banners. Turn your eyes from me; they overwhelm me. Your hair is like a flock of goats descending from Gilead. Your teeth are like a flock of sheep coming up from the washing. Each has its twin, not one of them is alone. Your temples behind your veil are like the halves of a pomegranate. Sixty queens there may be, and eighty concubines, and virgins beyond number; but my dove, my perfect one is unique, the only daughter of her mother, the favorite of the one who bore her. The maidens saw her and called her blessed; the queens and concubines praised her. Who is his that appears like the dawn, fair as the moon, bright as the sun, majestic as the stars in procession? I went down to the grove of nut trees to look at the new growth in the valley, to see if the vines had budded or the pomegranates were in bloom. Before I

realized it, my desire set me among the
royal chariots of my people.
Song of Solomon 6:4-12 (NIV)

Can you imagine what it would be like if our spouse or someone we loved spoke to us this way? Yet, this is how God sees us. The Scripture is a beautiful picture of a love relationship between two people, but it is also an allegory of the love relationship between God and each of us. My dove, my perfect one, is unique.

My personal portrait will be like no other. The way I am formed, the circumstances in my life, my facial expressions, hair color and my body, mind and soul all make me who I am. There is no one else like me, or like you. We are perfect and unique. Have you ever marveled at how God can take two eyes, a nose and a mouth and make each human being individual with their own identity? It's a miracle! We are miracles!!

Our lives and how we live them provide God with the colors needed to paint our individual masterpieces. There may be times when He has to paint over the mistakes (as we allow Him) we make but He always corrects with an attitude of love. It is so exciting to think that God is working in cooperation with me. He is painting my personal portrait, holding the brush ready as I provide him with the colors as I live my life. I am collaborating with God to do wonderful work for the kingdom. How wonderful!

> *Now if we are children, then we are heirs—heirs of God and co-heirs with Christ, if indeed we share in his sufferings in order that we may also share in His glory.*
> Romans 8:17 (NIV)

Does this passage prove that we are indeed co-heirs of the kingdom with Christ? If we share in his sufferings (carry our own cross), we will share in His glory.

One mistake that people make when viewing a painting is to walk up very closely and start trying to look at every little speck of paint the artist's brush has applied. To truly appreciate an impressionistic painting you must stand back and look at it from a distance. Look at the entire painting. View the artist's masterpiece from his perspective.

Have you ever tried to do something and someone is looking over your shoulder telling you how they would do it or what they think you are doing wrong. I've had this happen. It makes me want to scream.

My husband and I work together on a daily basis. Often times I will be typing something on the computer that has to do with our work as he will read what I am typing over my shoulder. The computer immediately recognizes when I make a grammatical error or misspell something. So does my husband! I often have to remind him I would prefer we finish the project, go over it together and then make the needed changes. This works in life and when painting.

If you are constantly looking at every little thing with a critical eye, you may actually miss the beauty of the picture. My art teacher used to look carefully, from a distance and then over my shoulder before pointing out my mistakes. I enjoy picturing God standing back and viewing my entire life before He steps up and looks over my shoulder to help correct my mistakes.

If I am a disciple of Jesus and His word is instilled in my Heart, my uniqueness will come out on my canvas of life in a way unlike any one else. I may have the same components as other human beings but I will not have the same DNA as anyone else. When we compare our talents with others we take away from the glory of God. He made us to be unique. The secret is to accept that uniqueness and be happy with who we are.

> *Jesus said: "And you shall love the Lord your God out of and with your whole heart and out of and with all your soul (your life) and out of and with all your mind (with your faculty of thought and*

your moral understanding) and out of
and with all of your strength. This is the
first and principal commandment. The
second is like it and is this, You shall love
your neighbor as yourself. There is no
other commandment greater than these.
Mark 12:30-31 (AMP)

Love your neighbor as yourself. In my opinion, not to love who we are is a sin. It says God created something less than perfect. We are human. There is always room for improvement in our lives. We shouldn't be looking at what we feel is wrong; we should instead appreciate our abilities and talents and cultivate them so we can have the character of Jesus. After all, we are made in His image.

We will often encounter obstacles in our lives that try to detour us from our true path. However, God will provide circumstances, people to encourage us and lead us, and the assistance of the Holy Spirit to direct us and help us complete our journey safely. Everything in our life will come together to complete our masterpiece brushed on our canvas personally by our Father.

We are assured and know that (God being
a partner in their labor) all things work
together and are (fitting into a plan) for
good to and for those who love God and

are called according to (His) design and
purpose.
Romans 8:28 (AMP)

My life was once a blank canvas but now reflects the image of Christ. It took planning, following the steps that had been laid out before me by Him who loves me, and the use of my God given talent to finish it. I'm pleased. It is exactly what I had hoped it would be.

God is still painting my personal masterpiece. I trust Him completely. He planned for me before I was born, He provided Jesus at the cross to cover my mistakes, and He lovingly and patiently applies pure color each day of my life. The construction has been laid; the yellow ochre (Holy Spirit) is at work and I have processed from dark to the light. The pure color (cross-hatching) has been laid on my canvas and my portrait is nearly complete. My hope is that when God stands back and looks at it He will see His reflection in me and know that I have provided Him with pure color for His undying love.

For now we see only a reflection as in a
mirror; then we shall see face to face. Now
I know in part; then I shall know fully,
even as I am fully known.
1 Cor. 13:12

Contact Information:

Barbara Lachance
Email:
barbara@generationalsolutionsllc.com

To order more copies of this book, please visit:

www.barbaralachanceministries.org

Made in the USA
Charleston, SC
09 July 2011